SANTA CLAUS FOR PRESIDENT

AARON BLANTON

Santa Claus for President

©2019 by Aaron Blanton
with Better Believe It Books

Hardback ISBN: 978-1-62020-967-7
Paperback ISBN: 978-1-62020-937-0
eISBN: 978-1-62020-963-9

INKSWIFT
GREENVILLE, SC 29601

Enjoy this tongue-in-cheek political rhyming book! Santa should run for President, but since he can't—Trump is the next best thing!

What if Santa left the job he's had for all these years? Imagine all the girls and boys and disappointed tears.

Instead of bringing presents each year on Christmas night, perhaps he ran for President. Maybe he just might.

Would he be republican or maybe democrat? Or would he wear a big blue coat with his old red hat?

If old St. Nick ran for President would some say he's pretentious or would the fact he's Santa Claus be a conflict of interest?

I can almost see it, the quarrelsome debates. Who can better dig up dirt on all his running mates?

Santa Claus, of course; he has a list, it's true, and tons of little elves to find out what they do.

With reindeer in his cabinet he could guide us straight. He could make us once again: America the great!

Everything that you just read was just a silly dream. But Santa Claus is busy so Trump's the next best thing.

Don't leave him milk and cookies 'cause Trump is on a diet and if you voted for him you might should keep it quiet. If "Naughty" knew you voted for Trump, they may just start a riot.

Santa Claus and Trump are sort of like the same, neither one of course is in it for the fame.

Whether you're a lefty or naughty little kid, this year instead of presents coal is what you'll get.

Now you know the truth, but I don't find it shocking. I think you would be mad, too, if coal was in your stocking.

You hear them singing loudly of their rumors of collusion, while their children sleeping soundly are awaken to confusion.

What happened to their gifts? What happened to their tree? Is that the kind of present that you want to give to me?

What happened to their laughter? What happened to their hope? All things to consider the next time that you vote!

Santa Claus for President, while that may sound just crazy. Are the leaders biased? Or maybe they're just lazy.

Keep in mind it could be worse with the Former secretary. The fact that she's still running free, I find kind of scary.

Now we know the Former party made Islam a deal. "Let's give Iran two billion cash!" Oh, man, are you for real? Did they kidnap Santa or at least his magic sack?

Or were they just that crazy to give a gift like that? Why be mad at Trump and shout and shake your fist? It's not his fault the lefties have topped the naughty list.

When Donald makes a deal with the likes of North Korea, he doesn't spend a U.S. dime and without the bloodshed either.

Some say Trump is naughty. He is a bit mischievous, but I prefer his antics over any of the previous.

A man who left the good life and his occupation, to now be dodging bullets aimed at his public reputation.

I guess that's just the thanks you get for global restoration, for economic growth, and jobs around the nation. So, you other voters save your breath and take a long vacation!

I'm perplexed with DACA and immigration, too. Don't you know the other guys sent all our jobs to you.

Santa flies around the world in just one Christmas night. I'm concerned if you're not home, your kids won't get their bikes.

Do the Elves a favor, so there won't be a mess. Go through the proper process if you want to change address.

Should I just keep writing, with more matters to undress, or simply put this rant to rest and say that I digress?

I think the subject matter should not be black or white. Color is not the answer when the question is wrong or right.

Let us unite our nation. Let us re-write the news. Let us direct our focus on the persecuted Jews.

God has blessed our country, a fact you can't refuse. If we forsake His people, it's our freedom we may lose.

Jesus is the answer, this is what I say! Only He can save us, so let Him light the way!

We finally have a leader who is fighting for believers. The uproar shouldn't shock you from the most vocal Deceivers.

There is no perfect President, I think we know that's true, but he continues fighting for the Christians and the Jews. He can count on my vote in the 2020, too!

No President is perfect, we all have our flaws, if only I could get my wish and vote for Santa Claus.

Then one day I called him, and this is what I said, "I put you on the ballot and you'll be running red!"

He hung up the phone, so then I called him back. I heard him mutter something about a missing magic sack.

Way to go you buffoon, you ruined it for us all! Why'd you have to go and tick off dear old Santa Claus?

Can't we find some common ground to find a resolution? Oh, I think I found it, it's called the Constitution.

I blame global warming on political pollution. Science finally found the cause of this deranged delusion.

That explains conspiracies of Russia-Trump collusion, divide and conquer tactics by the author of confusion.

You and I may disagree, but that's just my conclusion. You can thank me later, since I gave my contribution!

Opinions are like fingers and maybe even bottoms, some have less than others, but everybody's got'em.

I can't tell you what to think and neither can the news. Remember Santa's watching, and he knows just what you do.

Shakespeare said it once before, so I will say it, too. My favorite Christmas motto, "To thine own Elf be true!"

In the case of the corruption, we know who fits the shoe. The Inspector General report now confirms it, too.

Will anything become of this? I don't know. Do you? The left looks like an episode of Mister Magoo.

They're blinded by their bias with no regard for you. Hurry someone grab a broom and clean this filthy zoo.

This ain't your grandpa's party, so put them in their places. As far as I remember all the snakes belong in cages.

For all the common citizens who happen to be Blue, don't misunderstand me, these shots are not at you.

How can I explain this, so you will understand? These damaging illusions are called a sleight of hand, to redirect your focus so you won't see their plans. And YES, I want to ante up because I can see their hands!

With our trading upside down and our backs against the walls. What genius said, "We'll fix it! Let's just boycott plastic straws."

I'm with Nikki Haley, we all should be that bold. When the deck is stacked against you, just simply say I fold.

With cheaters at the table you have to take a stand, that's the only way for us to keep the upper hand.

To any bold believers, voice your righteous statements. If you don't it won't be long, your church might be your basements!

As for the Stormy Waters, Speaker pull her reins. We warned you of the side effects of too much sugar cane.

Someone check their meds, I think they've gone insane. When your party turns on you, there's always Trump to blame.

That's the thing with throwing dirt and with slinging sand. Regardless if you hit your target, you're left with dirty hands.

When I walk through the valley, I won't fear the evil, especially when evil is old, and it's feeble.

Try as you might to rally your people, I can fly higher than crows. I'm an eagle!

You must think it's Halloween, I don't know who you're trickin'. How dare you speak the word of God, when we all know you're Wiccan.

Good will always win; we've covered all the bases. That's why you wear a silly mask to hide your dumbfound faces.

You should have learned a lesson from Sodom and Gomorrah. We the people won't look back when God does destroy ya.

I suppose you live a sinful life and that's your naughty mission. You don't need mine or Santa Claus or any Judge's permission.

Naughty has mastered a dark dying art, in fact the first to earn the "The lying Purple Heart." Strike one, strike two, strike three you're through. It's no wonder Trump doesn't trust his intel community, when some sold them out with their testimony.

You know they should get some type of immunity, just give their indictment to the CROOKED secretary!

How do we live with the dark cloudy stench? The Republic of Santa's been put in a pinch, the culprit none other, "The party of Grinch."

Someone signed a guilty plea for things that aren't crimes. People please excuse me, I'm at loss for words to rhyme.

The founding fathers told us lady justice should be blind. That's not only Naughty, that's just wrong and bad combined.

Corruption's like a cancer that you hope would be benign. Cut the lies, you hypocrites, it's time you changed your mind.

Santa sends his little elves to make sure kids are nice. Donald Trump has helpers too, they're called police and ICE.

They both work hard to clean our streets at night when we're asleep. The others want to snuff them out while waging war on speech.

I'd hate to see them have their way, they'd put Trump in a peach. The matter that concerns me most is Naughty's over reach.

Kris Kringle fights cold weather with a smile upon his face, with a magic sleigh and reindeer he rewards the human race.

While Santa Claus is President, we'll take our fight to space. I can almost see it now the fear on Russia's face.

You may sometimes disagree with the President's positions, but you know he's doing something right to tick off many politicians.

J ustice Elf, you hit the nail with your opening statement. Silence swept around the room and across the nation.

I'm not surprised so many are willing to destroy, in fact they're bent on killing little girls and little boys.

Naughty, nearly fooled us amidst the cries and smiles, but Santa nearly fainted when he heard your flyer miles.

If you believe in what you see and trust them then so be it. But you can't fool me, I watch TV. I know acting when I see it.

It seems fit only Santa makes trade deals with Canada and knows to include Mexico. So, when they climb the wall, he'll give them a call, and know where their packages go.

All the smoke and mirrors merely prestidigitation, while the elves and Trump and Santa are clearly fighting for our nation.

Elf Ambassador's resignation, I said it was prophetic. I wrote it before you saw it. I wrote it before it happened. Mighty is the pen, mighty is the Lord, mighty is Jehovah, and mighty is the sword.

Aloha Pastor Brunson, you made it back for Christmas, your first one in two years. I hate to be the one to break it, but we face our greatest fears.

For you these should be cheerful times, a beautiful December. I fear this year our country's Christmas won't be quite what you remembered.

The future is at our door and bombers on the loose. Look who's finally interested in finding out the truth. Excuse me, while I speculate, don't mean to sound contrite. I say some conspired this, too, and quote me if I'm Right.

Armed with political pipe-bombs and they're trying to throw the fight. When will they finally realize two wrongs don't make a RIGHT?

Santa is going to shut it down if he doesn't get his wall. Compared to a hundred and fifty, five is pretty small.

Please don't go and make him mad, he won't be at the malls. Besides these guys don't even like how he decks the halls.

THE END

THE MORAL OF THE STORY IS THAT SANTA CLAUS AND PRESIDENT TRUMP HAVE MANY SIMILARITIES. THE MAIN ONE BEING THAT NOT EVERYONE BELIEVES IN THEM, BUT THOSE THAT DO OFTEN GET EXACTLY WHAT THEY ASK FOR.

I HOPE YOU ENJOYED THE READING AS MUCH AS I DID WRITING. IT'S ABOUT TIME WE HAD SOME FUN AND QUIT ALL THE FIGHTING!

For more information about
Santa Claus for President
and
Aaron Blanton
please contact:
Santa45president@gmail.com

www.ingramcontent.com/pod-product-compliance
Lightning Source LLC
LaVergne TN
LVHW072116070426
835510LV00002B/75